How to Treat a Book

by Amanda StJohn

illustrated by Bob Ostrom

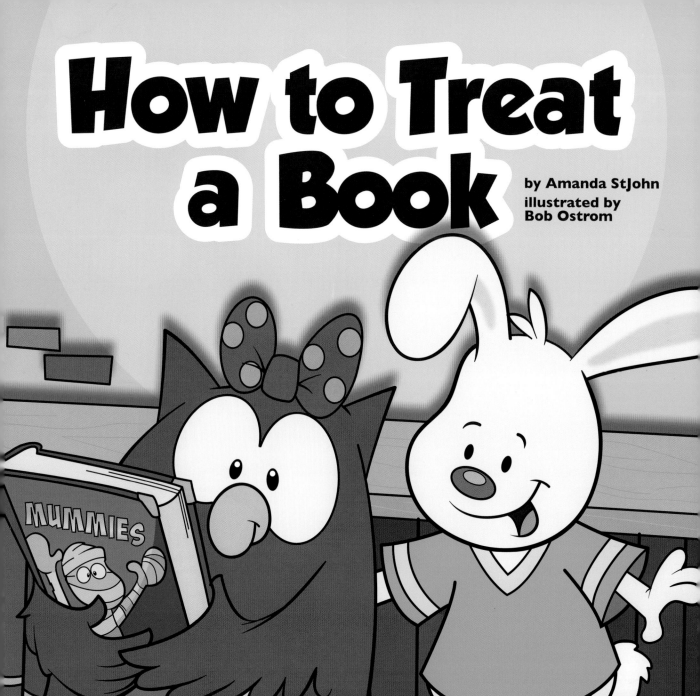

The Child's World®

Published by The Child's World®
1980 Lookout Drive • Mankato, MN 56003-1705
800-599-READ • www.childsworld.com

Acknowledgments
The Child's World®: Mary Berendes, Publishing Director
The Design Lab: Design and production
Red Line Editorial: Editorial direction

ISBN 9781614732525
LCCN 2012932863

Printed in the United States of America
Mankato, MN
November 2012
PA02156

About the Author

Amanda StJohn is an author and public librarian.
She's fascinated by singing frogs and animal tracks
and enjoys apricot tea and knitting.

About the Illustrator

Bob Ostrom is an award-winning children's
illustrator. His work has been featured in
more than two hundred children's books and
publications. When Bob is not illustrating children's
books you can usually find him in a classroom or
online teaching kids how to draw.

Opal and Stew visit the public library every Friday after school.

"Look at the new books," gasped Stew. "There's so many!"

Opal's eyes grew large. She saw a dark blue book. The book's **title** was written in gold letters. Opal sounded out the letters in a whisper. "Mm-uh-mm-ee-s."

"Mummies!" Opal shouted.

"Shhh," went a librarian.

"Sorry!" said Opal.

Opal loved mummies. She had a mummy lunch box and mummy posters in her bedroom.

"Let's borrow the mummy book," said Stew.

"Uh, no thanks," replied Opal.

Stew was confused. "Don't you want to read that new mummy book, Opal?"

"I . . . I do," stuttered Opal. "But I'm scared."

"You're scared of mummies?" squeaked Stew.

"No!" Opal giggled. "I, it's just . . . I've never borrowed a new book before. What if I ruin it?"

"Oh, Opal! We won't ruin it," smiled Stew. "I'll teach you how to treat books nicely."

First, Stew taught Opal was the parts of the book's body. "Books have a front cover, a back cover, and a **spine** in the middle. Covers protect a book's soft pages."

Opal was ready to hold the new book on mummies. She put her wingtip on the book's spine. She began to pull it off the shelf.

"Watch out," said Stew. "Push, don't pull."

"Huh?" Opal looked nervous.

"The spine protects a book's soft pages, but it can be broken. Don't pull the book off the shelf by the spine. Instead, push the books next to it—like this."

"I like that trick," said Opal.

Opal and Stew found a cozy place to sit down with the mummy book. The library was very busy. People of all ages were enjoying books, games, and computers.

"Look around," said Stew. "Watch how other people are treating books."

"Over there, " Opal clapped. "A badger is hugging his book while he walks along. I bet that's so he won't drop it."

"Right!" Stew exclaimed.

Opal saw Mrs. Moo was doing **research**. "Mrs. Moo has many books on her table, but they are neatly stacked. She is using bookmarks to save her favorite places. She has scrap paper for notes."

"Mrs. Moo always treats her books nicely," Stew agreed. "Imagine what it would be like if she didn't."

Opal and Stew pictured a naughty Mrs. Moo. This Mrs. Moo's books were scattered across the table and the floor. Some books were upside down, like tents. Naughty Mrs. Moo folded pages she liked. She colored in her library books. And she crinkled and tore pages when she turned them.

Stew shuddered. "From now on, I will turn my pages gently from corner to corner."

"I'll keep my books on the table, not the floor," nodded Opal.

Then, Opal needed to use the restroom. Stew said, "I'll hold the book for you, Opal. Books don't like to get wet."

"Oh, I think you're right." Opal remembered when her brother used his book as an umbrella. The cover got soaked and the pages wrinkled up like mummies.

Stew looked at his toes. "I once read a book in the bathtub. It slipped into the water and drowned."

Opal and Stew went to the front desk. Opal used her library card to borrow the book. "Would you like a bag for your books?" asked the librarian.

"We have book bags," said Stew. He unzipped his book bag. "Uh, oh." The inside of Stew's bag was wet. His water bottle had leaked.

Opal opened her book bag. It was stuffed with papers, books, and broken crayons. "Hmm," the librarian mused. "There's not much room in there."

Opal and Stew whispered together about what to do. Finally, Opal said, "May we please have a bag for our book?"

The librarian smiled and handed them a plastic bag. "Of course! That will keep your book safe."

When they arrived at Opal's house, Opal and Stew smelled something yummy. They left their book bags in the living room. Opal took her book out of its plastic bag and brought it with her into the kitchen.

"Cookies!" Opal clapped. Opal's mom had baked cookies with pink frosting. They were on a plate on the kitchen counter.

Opal put her book on the kitchen table, far from the cookies. She didn't want to get frosting on her book. Then she and Stew helped themselves to some cookies. After a hearty burp, Opal leapt up to get the mummy book.

"Freeze!" Stew called. "Dirty hands can ruin books." So Opal and Stew washed their hands with soap and warm water.

At last, Stew and Opal settled on the couch. They gently opened the mummy book. It was the best book Opal had ever seen. It had gold and silver letters. It had tons of facts. Best of all, it had a pop-up mummy.

"Aaaghh!" Stew yelped.

Opal's little brother, Owen, came to see the mummy book. "Mummy-mummy-mummy!" Owen poked the pop-up mummy again and again.

"Owen, no!" Opal cried.

Opal's mom saw Owen poking the mummy book. She swooped him up. "No, no, Owen," she said. "Treat books like friends. We don't poke our friends like that."

Stew turned the page of the mummy book. A large paw appeared on the page. It was Pansy, Opal's puppy. "Aaaghh!" screeched Opal. "Get off, get off, get off!"

Pansy's paw ripped the page. Opal began to cry.

"There, there," said Opal's mom. "What's wrong?"

"Pansy ripped my library book!" said Opal through her tears.

"We could try to tape it," suggested Stew.

"Thank you for that idea, Stew," said Opal's mom. "But the best thing to do is to tell a librarian what happened. Librarians use special book tape to fix rips and tears."

"Will they ever let me borrow books again?" Opal looked forlorn.

"Don't worry, Opal, they will," said Opal's mom. "But I'm afraid they will charge a **fine**. You'll have to pay with your allowance. But don't feel bad. The fine helps the library buy new books."

Stew sniffled. "I'm sorry I couldn't help you keep your new book safe, Opal. I never had a puppy jump on my books before."

Opal looked surprised. "But you did help me, Stew! Just think of all I learned!"

Glossary

fine (FINE): A fine is money you pay if you damage, lose, or return a library book late. Opal had to pay a fine for ripping her library book.

research (REE-surch): You do research to learn more about one topic or idea. Opal wanted to research mummies.

spine (SPINE): The part of a cover that helps a book stand up on the shelf. You can break a book's spine if you are not careful.

title (TYE-tul): The title is the name of the book. The title of Opal's book was *Mummies*.

Tips to Remember!

- Treat your book nicely.

- Hug your book to your chest to carry it without dropping it.

- Always wash your hands before handling books.

- Books don't like to get wet! Keep them away from sinks, bathtubs, and rain.

- Don't color or write in books.

- Use bookmarks.

Web Sites

Visit our Web site for links about library skills: childsworld.com/links

Note to Parents, Teachers, and Librarians: We routinely verify our Web links to make sure they are safe and active sites. So encourage your readers to check them out!

Books

Bennett, Elizabeth. *Watch Your Paws, Chester*. New York: Scholastic, 2011.

Bertram, Debbie. *The Best Book to Read*. New York: Dragonfly Books, 2011.

Morris, Carla. *The Boy Who Was Raised by Librarians*. Atlanta, GA: Peachtree, 2007.